The Imprint of a Yes

Deziree Paris

Copyright © 2023 by Deziree Paris

ISBN: 9798394494451

All rights reserved, including the right to reproduce this book or portions thereof of in any form whatsoever without prior written permission from the author. This includes storage in a retrieval system or transmission in any form. For information, contact the author via her website.

Contents

Chapter 1: Yes, Lord, Yes! 1

Chapter 2: My Soul Says Yes 2

Chapter 3: A Determined Yes 12

Chapter 4: Hold On Tight 23

Chapter 5: A Generational Yes 37

Dedication

I dedicate this book to several important people. First to my husband Stephen Gerrick for being the greatest supporter and purpose-pusher. To my first baby love Stephen Ezra, for being the motivation I need to build a better future. You will experience the rewards of my labor. To my mom Pamela Jean for teaching me that if I am real with God, He will be real with me. Then to Vassie Lean, Ethel Lee, and Vassie Anne for being the blueprint and beacon of light to my life.

Introduction

From the moment we are born, we are shaped by the words from our parents' or guardians' mouths that give us language. The words we possess have more power than can really be articulated. You can create the future you have always dreamt of and desired if you tailor your words to create the unseen. We are creative beings, designed after the image and likeness of the God who created nothing into something by speaking it into existence. We are to be mirrors of the One who created us.

If God said, "Let there be light" and there was light, in the same way, we can say, "Let there be prosperity in all facets of my life," because the scripture tells us, "I wish above all things that you may prosper and be in health, even as your soul prospers" (3 John 1:2). We don't have creative ability by our own power, but because we are one in the Spirit with Jesus, and He is one with God the Father. You have the authority through the risen Savior, our Lord Jesus Christ. Since Jesus has done all the work, we only need to come into agreement with the plan and purpose for our lives that comes by the renewing and washing of the mind through the water of the word. We can become new creatures in Christ Jesus, but we must agree to the new life transformation.

When you are in agreement with the Creator of the Universe, you are giving Him permission to mold you by any means necessary and form you into His image and likeness. This would be like a potter with a handful of clay, ready to convert it into a masterpiece shaped by diligent hands. An experienced potter, especially in ancient times, would begin to spin their clay on a wheel. Water would be added to make sure it was soft enough to knead. The clay would be spun and kneaded simultaneously, causing it to be shaped and formed into the image that was in the mind of the potter. The clay did not try to stop the process or spin in the opposite direction. Yet, the clay was submitted to the process of becoming the manifested idea of the creator.

The war we are actively participating in daily is the one for our Yes. We are physical beings in a world that is first spiritual. The spirit realm cannot intertwine with the physical realm if there isn't a covenant made by way of agreement. "Yes" is the word of agreement. It's the word of partnership and collaboration granted. God has given us the grace we need to come into agreement with Him. When approaching a God who is holy and perfect in all His ways, it can seem intimidating to come into His presence. Yet, because of the sacrifice of our Lord Jesus Christ, we can boldly come before the throne of grace. You get to choose who to come into agreement with.

Your Yes has so much power that the enemy will try to deceive you and scheme his way into having you come into agreement with him. There will come a moment in your time of worship, whether it be privately or corporately, where the presence of God manifests Himself to you and bids you to agree with Him. Do not take these moments for granted or make them an emotional experience but have a heart that is open without fear to surrender to the plan and purpose of God through a yes.

When you want something new, you must be willing to try something new. The journey God is taking you on will be one that is tailor-made to a scenic route, a journey that could have only been orchestrated by the Omnipotent God. This does not mean that the way is easy, but it does mean that no matter the circumstances that can come your way, "all things are working together for your good..." (Romans 8:28). There isn't one story, one experience, one testimony you have that God won't use. It is all meant to give Him glory, and He allows you to benefit. But to get to the expected end, you must start with a real yes.

Since the enemy is a copycat, he will attempt to pervert your godly identity into a devilish identity. An identity that is represented by the father of lies. When you come into agreement with the adversary, the identity that begins to form in you is one full of lies: about your purpose, your future, and your identity. The enemy does not want to see you become all that God has spoken for you to be. The enemy knows that God has made you a solution to a problem in the earth and that if you come into agreement with the Father you will accomplish great exploits and advance the Kingdom of God. Coming into agreement with the Author and Finisher of your faith means dying to yourself, declining your own selfish desires to experience God's desire for you. I believe with all my heart that the desire God has for my life far surpasses the grandest vision or dream I could ever have.

Be encouraged to know that the limitless God has a plan and a purpose for you. You are not a mistake, nor were you an accident, but instead you were crafted by the hand of God for such a time as this. I believe if you are reading this book, you are a trailblazer in your family, in your industry, or in your sphere. Your Yes is the power behind the wealth in your bloodline for generations to come. Your Yes will unlock generational blessings for the ones who will come after you. The purpose of God for your life is more than you can imagine, and He needs an unrestricted Yes to Him. Don't fight Him during the process, no matter how much pressure is being applied to you.

This Yes that God is asking for is to brand your life, the way an owner would brand their livestock as a way to identify their property. So is the effect of the imprint branding your life by giving God a Yes that will identify you to Him like no other. Your Yes to God is what makes you unique. There are people all over the world who desire influence, platform, and notoriety, but will not submit to the processing of the Lord. These people will always be able to pour out from their gifting but will miss the secret ingredient to make any of God's things work, which is His partnership. Your idea will only go so far without the endorsement of God. You may reach a few people, but you won't reach the masses, because you aren't in agreement.

My journey of giving God a Yes literally took me across the country. I was born and raised in California, and I had no idea I would ever leave the beautiful Sunshine State. You know that popular song "It Never Rains in Southern California?" Well, it does rain. I can recall the first time I ever gave God my real Yes, and the journey it took me on and is still taking me on. I was a junior in college, and when I tell you I had the "college experience," I mean we went to club Salsa on Thursday night, Frat party on Friday night, went party-hopping on Saturday night, then slept in all day Sunday. I did this with my closest friends for the first two years of school.

By the time I came to myself, I was worn out. I was empty, void, and feeling so unworthy. I spent so much time trying to have the college experience I saw on TV shows, but I didn't know I was doing this because I didn't feel loved. I was out there searching for love in all the wrong places. I was looking for it with partying, I was looking for it in weed, I was looking for it in casual sex, I was looking for it in random strange men on Craigslist. I was looking for something to fill this nagging void, yet after I did my best to fill it, I found myself emptier than when I started. The only thing I knew how to do was go back to God.

I am what some may consider a pew baby. I used to sit on the front row with my great-grandmother, who was the Evangelist at my little storefront church growing up. I can remember always hearing my grandmother say, "If you train up a child in the way they should go, when they get older they won't depart from it. They may stray for a while, but after a while, the Holy Ghost will get them." I experienced what she meant when she would say that the Holy Ghost will "get them." The Holy Spirit was wooing me back to God during college, and I didn't realize it. Every time I found myself in a scary situation—and there were several occasions during college when this happened—the Holy Spirit made a way for me to escape, and kept me from hurt, harm, and danger.

I don't know what exactly happened to make me eventually see it, but I finally had a Prodigal Son moment, and I came to myself. I knew I needed God. I didn't want to do this thing called life alone anymore. I understood that in my adult years, I had to give God my own Yes. I could no longer live off the Yes my grandmother and great-grandmother had made to God. I realized this was a personal thing I had to make between me and the Father. I had already accepted Jesus into my life, so I wasn't a sinner in the aspect that I didn't confess or believe that Jesus Christ was Lord. However, I had never received the Holy Spirit with the evidence of speaking in tongues like is taught all throughout the New Testament.

I went home to visit family one weekend, and after the First Lady of the church preached her message, she made a call that anyone who wanted to receive the Holy Spirit to come to the altar. So, I did. I went up there with my arms lifted, and I stood there. Time went by, the altar call ended, and I didn't receive the Holy Spirit. I went back to my seat mad. I felt like that lady was guilty of false advertising. Why say to come up there if I wasn't going to receive Him? My grandmother sat next to me and said, "Baby, you can't be upset. It might've not been your time yet. When the Holy Spirit is ready for you to receive Him, you'll receive Him with no limits."

What she said weighed on my heart as I traveled back to my college town and stayed with me all that week. That following Sunday I went back to the church I was actively visiting at the time. At that 6 p.m. service, the pastor concluded his message and opened the altar. I knew I needed some prayer because I had been toiling within myself for months. So I went up to the altar worker and she proceeded to ask me what I needed prayer for. I really couldn't articulate it. I felt like I needed prayer for everything. There wasn't one aspect of my life I felt didn't need prayer. I sincerely felt like I was in turmoil, like I was at a fork in the road concerning my life and destiny.

She then asked me, "Have you ever been baptized?" I initially thought this was an odd question to ask when I had come up for prayer. Yet, after all the wayward living I had done over those last three years, I felt dirty, and a baptism to get cleaned by God didn't sound like a bad idea. So I said why not. I had been baptized at an early age with my cousins, but I had never been baptized with an understanding of what it really meant to go down into a watery grave and then be raised to a new life. So, she proceeded to take me up the stairs to the baptism area and went over a few scriptures in reference to what was about to take place. I can remember the nerves and anticipation rising in my heart.

When I got into the baptism pool, I had one of the shortest yet most real conversations with God I have ever had. I was desperate for Him to answer and show up for me. I said in that pool with the most sincere heart, "God if you don't fill me today, it must not be meant for me to be filled." The Elder was reciting, "Upon the confession of your faith in the death, burial, and resurrection of our Lord and Savior Jesus Christ, I indeed baptize you in the name of Jesus for the remission of your sins, and you shall receive the gift of the Holy Spirit."

When he dunked me in the water, I came up speaking in tongues. I was full of the Holy Ghost; I couldn't stop praising God in my new heavenly language. I was drunk in the Spirit. I was trying to get out of the baptism pool speaking in tongues. I was changing out of those drenched clothes still speaking in tongues. I drove home, called my grandmother, and said, "Mom-mom, I got the Holy Ghost" and proceeded to speak in tongues, and my grandmother did on the phone, too. It was a moment engrained in my history. That Yes to God changed the trajectory of my life and took me on a path called risky faith.

I believe as you read this book, you will discover that the journey you are on is because you gave God a real Yes. When you give God a Yes, He will take you on a path to imprint that Yes into you, so you can stand during any trial and not revert your yes to God and make it a no to Him. The fight of this life is one for our agreement. You will either come into agreement with God or the enemy. Those are the two choices we have. Light or darkness. Holiness or deviousness. We must choose, and what I realize is when I don't choose God, I automatically choose what is enmity to God. I pray that by the time you finish this book, you will make your election sure. I pray that you will stand the process of allowing God to imprint your Yes into you.

Chapter 1

Yes, Lord, Yes!

I took an Intercession course at my church back in 2018, and it was taught by one of the most dynamic Intercession teachers of our times by the name of Broderick McBride. I can recall being in this class one Sunday morning before the main worship service. We were in a newly acquired property for the ministry and there were still a ton of renovations needed. So the intercessors would gather behind the sanctuary in these two adjoining rooms. That room would be hot, and the floors would squeak when you stepped on them. This particular day was seemingly different, however, even though it was in the same room and at the same time as our previous gatherings. Something wasn't the same. The atmosphere was different. Maybe it was the reality that we were in a building, or perhaps it was one of those "new levels, new devils" types of situations. All I knew was that there was something different in the familiar gathering space that now seemed to be unfamiliar.

Pastor Broderick began to tell a story I had never heard before. I grew up in the Church of God in Christ which was founded by Bishop Charles H. Mason. My little storefront church located in South Central Los Angeles used to sing "Yes, Lord" every Sunday to start the service. We would have Sunday school first, then during the fifteen-to-twenty-minute break in between, my cousins and I would walk across the street to the local corner store for 25-cent Now and Later candies (the watermelon ones were my favorite), a 25-cent bag of chips, and a 50-cent bag of Grandma's mini-cookies. We would sit in the kitchen and eat our snacks, and when we started to hear the deacon sing "Yes, Lord" we knew it was time to finish what we were eating and go into the sanctuary.

So when Pastor Broderick began to tell this story, I felt connected to it because of my upbringing. He began to tell the story about how Bishop Mason grew up in a time that was heavily segregated, and racial oppression was at its peak. Bishop Mason had been known in his Southern town and the regions around for gathering people of all races together to worship God. The bishop didn't just have five or ten people following his ministry, but hundreds and even thousands. It was so widespread and everyone knew about the work Bishop Mason was doing, gathering whites and blacks together. Eventually, Klansmen began to show up and intimidate him. They tried to force him to stop gathering the people and stop integrating blacks and whites together. However, Bishop Mason was on fire for God, after being filled with the Holy Spirit during the famous Azusa Street Revival of 1906 to 1915. He believed all people should come together and worship our One God together regardless of race or economic background, as he had seen in Los Angeles during the revival. So, he continued to preach the gospel and the people continued to gather.

One night, as the bishop and his family were in their home sleeping, a group of hooded men came to the bishop's home, banged on the door, and demanded he come out. After calming his wife and daughter, he proceeded outside to confront these men. They rushed to grab him, tying him up by his feet and hands. They proceeded to tar and feather him, then took him to the backwoods to bury him alive. As they dragged the bishop into the dark woods, his wife and daughter gathered themselves, frantic and afraid of what was happening before their eyes. In the midst of not knowing what to do, they remembered what their husband and father had taught them, which was to pray. She said, "Lord, where is my husband? Lord, where did they take him?" The Holy Spirit began to lead them into the woods.

The Imprint of a Yes

As they followed the prompting of the Holy Spirit they never stopped praying, "Lord, where did they take him? Show us the way." As they got deeper into the woods they began to hear a low and faint voice singing, "Yes, Lord. Yes, Lord. Yes, Lord. Yes, Lord. Yes, Lord." When they heard the voice, they began to praise God and walked even faster in that direction. They were in the dark amongst the unfamiliar deep woods, but they didn't stop following the voice. As they continued into the woods, the voice got louder and they begin to hear, "Have your way, have your way, have your way, have your way, have your way." The women found the shallow grave containing the buried Bishop Mason, got on their hands and knees, and began to dig him out. Once they reached the wooden box he had been put in and threw out the last bit of dirt that had kept him in the ground, he jumped up out of that grave with his hands lifted and sang, "I love you, Lord. I love you, Lord. I love you, Lord. I love you, Lord. I love you, Lord. I love you, Lord."

Anytime God gives you a mission in the earth that will disrupt the cultural norms, God will require a real Yes from your heart. This Yes is not a shallow saying, but it is the agreement between earth and heaven, and our Yes is the conduit in which heaven manifests itself on earth. Bishop Mason and this story show us that as you do the will of God, there will be people who will hate you, some who will try to intimidate you, and some who might even try to bury you in a shallow grave. But their contention against you isn't something that is flesh and blood, but a war in the spirit for the advancement of the kingdom of God. This is why God requires a real Yes from us before He gives us the complete details of what that yes will entail. I say a "real Yes" because we have all had times when we give God a conditional Yes. This means I will tell God yes, as long as the situation stays favorable. Or I will say yes to God as long as I get something out of the deal. Or even, I will give God a Yes as long as I don't have to be too uncomfortable.

But what happens when your yes costs you your life? This is the real Yes I am speaking of, because when you submit yourself with a "Yes Lord, Yes," you are saying, "I give You complete control over everything." From your timeline to your desires, how you want it to happen, and even your geographical location. This is why when you give God a true Yes from your heart, He begins to take you through the process of imprinting that Yes into your heart. When the Yes is imprinted into your heart, you are able to stand through persecution and not fold under pressure. The process of this imprint is to give you the power to endure.

The Imprint of a Yes

There are many who tell God yes in the moment because they have the emotional sensation that leads them to say yes with their lips but not their heart. So when the first wave of inconvenience arises they take back their Yes, and remove themselves from the process of having their Yes imprinted into them. Your future needs you to stay on the potter's wheel. What would have happened if Bishop Mason had given up his Yes to the Lord when he was facing humiliation and death? The birth of the Church of God in Christ might not have been. A little girl in that storefront church would have never been introduced to "Yes, Lord" at the beginning of service, and she would have never been groomed at a young age to tell the Lord Yes.

As a child, I didn't understand what it meant to tell the Lord Yes, but as I heard this story many years later, it seemed to come around full circle. I found myself in a different state, part of a church that God told me He was sending me to, all because I told the Lord Yes. When you surrender your life to God and tell Him Yes, He will take you to places you never thought you would have gone, to be around people you didn't think you were called to, and have you plant roots in spaces that seem to be foreign. Yet, it's all a part of the plan for God to imprint a Yes in you, so to have you flexible to both His plan and way. Many people are fine with the plan of God but tend to not want the way of God.

The real Yes you give to God will be imprinted into your memory, the same way this encounter has been engrained in mine. After Pastor Broderick told this story, the glory of God descended, and many intercessors gave God a real Yes. That Yes for me might have been different than the others in there. But that Yes for me was not just to that church and what they were building, but to the mandate God had planned for my life, and I didn't want to run from it or give only half of myself any longer. I wanted to give God an all-in, "I won't look back" type of Yes. Over those next few years, I experienced persecution and ridicule, as well as being shunned, disrespected, misunderstood, and overlooked. But even amongst quarantine and the pandemic, God took me on a journey to have the Yes I gave Him to be so engrafted into my being that nothing could cause me to turn my back on Him and His will for my life. This is what God desires for you. The power to endure the test and trials of life comes by way of the power of the Holy Spirit working on the inside of you. But the Holy Spirit can't work if you don't come into agreement with Him by way of your Yes.

This real Yes is the first Yes to start the process of really becoming. It's the Yes that tells God, "I want to be all You designed me to be and in every area." I want to live in the dream God has for my life. So that may mean I have to be pushed aside

The Imprint of a Yes

for a season by the ones I love, for Him to promote me amongst strangers. The processing of a God Yes will take you through uncharted territory because it's not the way often traveled. We live in a time when people love their way. We've all heard that saying, "It's my way or the highway." This statement is problematic for one being processed by God because more times than not you won't get your way. If having your way is what fuels you to give God a Yes, you might as well keep it, because you won't be able to have both your way and God's way.

The scripture tells us in Isaiah 55:8-9, "For my thoughts are not your thoughts, neither are your ways my ways, saith the Lord. For as the heavens are higher than the earth, so are my ways higher than your ways, and my thoughts than your thoughts." God has a way of utilizing our Yes in the sequence of events that occur after, to get His will accomplished in us and through us. If God were to tell us that after we say Yes, we'd lose our job, our dog will die, someone will steal our identity, our car battery will die, you will have a falling-out with your best friend, you will experience heartbreak, and only then you will recover it all, some of us wouldn't tell God yes, even if we do recover it all in the end. We are a generation that tries to avoid getting hurt at all costs.

But what if the only way that God can process out of you the toxic behavior of double-mindedness and self-sabotage is to allow you to experience temporary hurt, so you can experience eternal reward? As unknown as a Yes may seem in the moment, God has already orchestrated what the expected end will be. God isn't making it up as we go; it's already mapped out. He is so intentional about what coming into agreement will yield for the earth that He wrote out the end from the beginning. Our job is simple: stay on the path. What would have happened if Peter, after stepping off the boat and beginning to walk on the water, had kept his focus on Jesus and not the storm around him? Maybe he would have reached Jesus, or maybe he would have walked all the way to the other side of the lake, or maybe other disciples would have joined him and gotten out of the boat too. But that's not what we read; instead, Peter got distracted and began to sink, but before the water could overtake him, Jesus came and rescued him.

Jesus doesn't only want to rescue you, but He wants to partner with you to do greater works. Yes, Jesus is our savior, but He also wants to be your friend. I don't know about you, but I have fun with my friends. We make memories and have experiences together. This is what Jesus wants for us. He wants to take our relationship to the next level. He wants us to experience life with Him, not just as our Savior but as our friend. What sort of exploits could we accomplish for his glory if we would do it from the perspective of being a friend of God? It's a journey, not a sprint. Many fall by the wayside because they want to quickly run with Him instead of slowly travel with Him. So when He is processing the Yes you give, expect to journey with God.

The Yes you give God isn't just for you but for your bloodline, your children, and your children's children. It's your legacy and your inheritance. Giving God a real Yes will leave an imprint on the earth that will last for generations to come. Not because we are so grand, but because we found the power in agreement between heaven and earth in the simple three-letter word "YES." You can change the trajectory of a generation if you come into agreement with God, and not just come into agreement but mean it with your whole heart. Give God a real Yes, and offer God no resistance to His plan, purpose, and will. Because you don't know what little boy or girl your "Yes, Lord, Yes" will touch a hundred years from now, but God does. So today, tell the Lord Yes.

Chapter 2

My Soul Says Yes

You are a spirit that has a soul, which lives inside a body. Your soul houses the intellect, emotions, imagination, and will. I mention this at the top of the chapter because I want to teach you that giving God a real Yes will come through your soul. Oftentimes when we hear the phrase "tell the Lord Yes," we are in the praise and worship part of church service. You know, the part when the praise and worship leader yells into the microphone to the congregation, "Lift up your hands and tell the Lord yes" while singing their slow song they call worship. In the midst of the intense emotions, many follow the misunderstood command as if they were playing "Simon Says," making a declaration they have no intention of keeping past the threshold of the sanctuary. Many think the lifting of your hands is just part of the antics that go along with church culture.

The Imprint of a Yes

However, when done with full understanding, your uplifted arms can be like antennas in the earthly realm, getting direct reception from the Heavenly Father. When you do things in the body of Christ without understanding, you are doing the exterior works but don't perceive the reward of agreement. When you lift your hands, whether in worship on a Sunday morning or in your kitchen washing dishes on a Tuesday, it's a physical sign that says "I agree and I receive." This is what that looks like. The Spirit of the Lord says, "I'm sending you to nations so my glory can be manifested in the earth." The intellectual portion of the soul receives the word. It processes the word for the author and the truth that's embedded in it. Then it sends the word into the imagination of the mind, which reasons with the word on the probability that it could happen for you. Then the intellect sends the findings over to the emotions. The emotions allow the dominant feeling to respond. So if your soul is full of fear, self-doubt, rejection, disbelief, and disappointment, your response will correlate. It only takes a moment for the intellect and emotions to cast their vote to the will. This portion of your soul takes all the information in, with consideration of your past and if you're willing to take a risk, then decides.

Our will often wants to play it safe. It would rather have the route of least resistance, challenges, disappointment, difficulties, and obstacles. This is why being delivered from a spirit of fear is necessary for your future because you can't get there by faith if fear is keeping you stuck in place. Fear wants you to come into agreement that you won't succeed. Fear tries to get you to come into agreement with the thought that you will fail. God wants to take you to a place where you live the dream God has for you, but the way to get there will be full of risk. You won't have control, you won't know the way, and it will not be the fastest and most convenient route. But it will lead you to destiny with your purpose.

So the decision-making part of your soul is the will, and the will determines the way. Once the will has made the decision on whether it will walk in the Spirit or live in the flesh, then the body responds accordingly. After the words have been cross-examined by all the portions of the soul, it sends the decision of how to react to the word in the body. Then the body raises its arms and stretches its hands to the sky and says, "Yes Lord, I agree with your word in the Spirit realm, and I receive the manifestation of the word in the earthly realm."

Every part of your soul has to say yes. I remember hearing my grandmother (who I affectionately call Mom-mom) pray on many occasions, "My soul says yes." This prayer would be accompanied by groanings which I now understand was the Holy Spirit making intercession on her behalf. I believe there are times when your faith, which is strengthened by the Spirit, can be so strong that it overrules your soul, automatically coming into agreement with the will of God as soon as the word comes from the Father, without any explanation or reasoning. This happens when you live a life that says Yes to God. It doesn't matter what the Lord wants, or how He may ask for it. He has permission to be the captain of this body to do His will.

When you are a passenger on a plane, you do not go and knock on the pilot's door and ask the captain what route he's taking to get you to your destination. Most people aren't a pilot, and the average person doesn't know how to navigate the sky. Our view and expertise are limited to ground transportation. The pilot knows how to navigate the flight in such a way as to get you to your destination as swiftly and safely as possible. So that might mean changing elevations to be on a stream of wind that will give a tailwind to speed things up. Or they may have to fly a longer course in another direction that might seem out of the way. But the captain knows that in order to fly with the wind for a safe and smooth flight, they may have to take the long way. God is the same way. He knows how to steer our lives in such a way that gets us to our destiny with our characters matured, our emotions refined, and our gifts sharpened. So there is no need to question God the Captain because we are in good hands.

The soul is the treasure the Lord placed in our earthen vessel. It's the unique part of who we are individually. This soul is what separates humans from angels. The soul has the capability to change. Angels were made perfect by God in the heavenly realm and have no need to change. We were made by God in the corruptible realm, so we will forever be changing. The enemy sees that in this earthly realm, changes can be made at every moment. You get to make a choice during every experience that comes your way, and every decision leads you closer to an outcome based on the decision.

If you want to lose weight, you change your eating habits and you get active—not for just one day, but over days, weeks, and months—and you will see yourself going in the direction of the decision that you made to become healthy. You lose weight and the body starts to change. When making decisions that positively impact your being, it opens you up to receive help from the angels that are assigned to you. These are the moments when you took time to be intentional during your prayer time with God. The moments you go work out of obedience to a command God gave you about your physical health. This opens you up to the

The Imprint of a Yes

partnership of God that is accompanied by benefits for your obedience to Him.

In the same way, we can come in agreement with God, however, choosing to do the opposite can cause us to come into agreement with the enemy. You can come into agreement with the enemy by burning sage and praying to your ancestors because you believe Jesus needs help to fulfill your wishes and prayers. Things of this nature can open you up to the spirit of the occult. This spirit can oppress you by sending tormenting spirits to intimidate you with fear. When you are fearful and anxious, your soul is being fed by a spirit of heaviness that will keep you bound. If you have ever experienced a time in your life (or maybe are experiencing it now) when it seemed like you were afraid of everything—a fear of succeeding, a fear of being rejected, a fear of failing—it can feel like everything is against you. But you don't have real proof that there is something physically opposing you. This is how you know there is a demonic spirit that could be oppressing you.

It's not just because of agreement to occult activity, but it's also opened by the negative decisions we make. God could have given you instructions to do a task, but because you didn't want to be the one God used, you didn't do it. So the door for a rebellious spirit to enter is agreed upon. Then, when you feel like your peace has been disturbed and you can't focus on completing a task, it's because that spirit is oppressing you to not accomplish anything in the earth. It will strip away your peace and cause you to feel like you aren't yourself, because the truth is, when we aren't doing the will of God we aren't our true selves. Jesus came to set us free from these demonic forces that would try to keep us earthbound when God has destined us for a new life that is more abundant. His sacrifice and finished work give us the power to command demonic spirits to leave our lives. They are structured spirits and have been setting up systems in the souls of believers for ages.

The power of God through Jesus Christ can eradicate all demonic spirits. The name of Jesus has that much power. No matter how many generations a spirit goes back in the bloodline, Jesus can go all the way back to the fall of Adam to cleanse your soul from demonic agreements that were made. When deliverance takes place and those demonic oppressors have been evicted, the residue must be washed away by the water of the Word. This is where the soul healing begins. This is where the Father shows you the lie that was spoken, and reveals there has been a truth you have never seen before that's always been there. The soul must be healed and filled back up with the Holy Spirit. The soul goes on an inner healing journey with the Holy Spirit. The Spirit of God walks with

The Imprint of a Yes 18

a person through their past to walk into their future. The healing of the soul is what fuels the soul to give God a Yes. The Yes wouldn't come from the emotions that change with the feeling of the moment. But the soul says Yes with the agreement of the whole being from a sober place of faith in God.

    I attended the very first cohort of The Prayer Institute with Dr. Juanita Bynum. She taught through a portion of the brain that held the soul, and how the mind works together with the soul and prayer. When you have experienced traumatic events in your life, if you reflect back you might have thought at the time they were normal. You may have been brought up by a grandparent; your parents might have been in and out of your life. This is traumatic. I know in this generation, people believe the word "traumatic" is overused. However, the word is only being overused in our generation and not necessarily by any other. There are other generations that believe that when a young child is molested in the family house, they are supposed to remain silent and "let what happens in this house stay in this house." Or maybe you only found out in your twenties that you have other siblings because your father had a secret family on the other side of town. This is traumatic. Or maybe you have experienced being overlooked or misunderstood because of your gender, age, body, or ethnicity. This is traumatic.

Situations that people deem to be normal in actuality have been doorways for demonic oppressors to keep you captive in the cages of unforgiveness, shame, depression, heaviness, regret, or abandonment. The power and love of Jesus have the ability to remove every spirit that would try to keep you bound. Once these hindrances have been removed, the inner healing work begins, because the real damage is from the lies that were believed by you. The spirit that has been in charge of telling you the lie that no one will ever choose you can be removed easily by the name of Jesus because He did the work on the cross. But our job is to go to the place of vacancy and partner with the Holy Spirit on the clean-up process. This means identifying what lie or belief this strongman was responsible for, then allowing the Holy Spirit to tell you how to fill it with the truth from His Word, which is that God loves you so much that He sent His only begotten son so that we might have a relationship with the perfect God.

You are loved by God and He chose you. Before you were in your mother's womb, He knew you. Now every time a situation occurs where you may be vying with another person applying for the same position as you, which triggers you into believing the old lie that no one will ever choose

The Imprint of a Yes 20

you, the Holy Spirit will bring to your remembrance that you are loved by God and chosen by Him. You must come into agreement with the true Word God has spoken about you. This takes time because you are building a new muscle. Strength training consists of consecutive repetitions of an exercise with the progression of more resistance. You are training your mind to believe the word God has spoken over you. This is why the psalmist said that we must meditate on His Word day and night. This starts a chain reaction with the other portions of your soul.

As you start to think differently, your emotions are challenged to respond differently as well. You will start to be filled with emotions that are characteristic of the Holy Spirit, like joy. For the joy of the Lord is our strength. What was once filled with heaviness and regret, along with shame, will be converted to joy, victory, thanksgiving, and gratitude. As inner healing takes place, we must submit our emotions to the Father so He can teach us through the Holy Spirit on how to be in control of our emotions and use them for the intent God made them, to experience life. God gave us emotions, so we are able to be as multidimensional as Himself. We can feel and experience life on a number of levels. To be able to be in any situation and still be content. In a situation that would cause others to crumble under the weight, you will be the one to find joy during the storm.

God created emotions for us to use, but not be led by them. As your emotions heal and submit, your imagination heightens to godly connectivity. What was once a creative blockade becomes an imagination oasis. It's in this space that your creative nature has unlimited possibilities. This is where the blank canvas receives its blueprint. When your imagination is healing, you will be able to see the word the Lord speaks to you, like a picture playing in your mind. Your imagination will allow you to see what it would look like to go to foreign nations and experience the presence of God manifest. If you can see it, then you will see it. You have to see God's vision in the invisible realm in order to experience it in the natural realm. Some of you haven't been dreaming big enough. What you want to see is too small for what God has in store for you. You aren't seeing your future clearly. You aren't perceiving your identity correctly. There is so much more to you than meets the eye. God handcrafted you with everything you need to accomplish His vision for your life, in your treasure called the soul. This part of your imagination is where witty ideas and uncommon inventions are created. You need your imagination revived. God can heal it.

Once all of these components have been touched by the finger of God, the will starts to experience overdrive. This is when the will blindly comes into agreement with God. The spirit of Grace may tell you in your private prayer time that He is about to launch you into full-time entrepreneurship. As soon as these words hit your ears, by faith you say, "Yes, Lord." In times past, if you would have heard this word with your unhealed soul, it would have you in fear. But when you are in the healing process, experience by experience you are getting a chance to strengthen up. This strength gives you confidence in the power and intentions of God towards you. Knowing that if God said He will do it, He will fund it, send the people for it, increase it, grow it, protect it, and keep it. Because where God gives the vision, He provides provision. So you live in the lane that says, "He is the leader and I'm following His lead," like a GPS to a predestined location.

Chapter 3

A Determined Yes

When I was in the 9th grade, I experienced a traumatic event that changed my life forever. I was on spring break during my first year of high school. I remember being so excited, because I would watch all the Disney Channel shows that portrayed high school spring break being the time of the characters' lives. I had high hopes of my first spring break being like an early 2000s TV sitcom, but instead, it turned into a Greek tragedy. On March 29th, 2006, I was in my room while my grandmother was cleaning the house, and I heard a scream from my grandmother that I had never heard before, one that haunted my dreams for years. I ran to the living room to see what was going on and watched my grandmother run out the front door, dropping the house phone in the middle of the floor with a distant voice still speaking on the other end.

I picked up the phone and said hello. The lady's voice on the other side asked if I was related to Levi Dukes. I replied that yes, that was my daddy. She asked if I was 18. I was not but I urgently responded, "He's my dad. What's going on?"

The doctor on the other end proceeded to tell me that he had expired while he was living in Atlanta and I was in California. To hear that he died in a hospital room alone grieved my heart to the point that it shut my heart off, and for a long time afterward I lived like a zombie, there but not there. In my mind, I could not get the word "expired" out of my head. Milk expires, not people, I remember proclaiming. For the next two years, I had convinced myself the reason why I hadn't heard from my dad was because he was upset with me about my poor grades.

Delusional and full of unprocessed grief, I kept moving forward, because the world doesn't stop just because a person stops living. I had to keep pushing. A few months later, my dad's only sister started going through chemotherapy for ovarian cancer. For the next year I would share a room with her, and I saw the cancer overtake her body. Yet she had a supernatural strength that only God could have given her because she would have the best attitude and gratitude for the goodness of God. There was a time she was in the hospital and the bishop brought her communion, and she had been witnessing to her nurses in such a way that they wanted to join in on communion too. She died later that year at the age of 44. My dad was also 44 when he passed.

By the time I was in my senior year of high school, my grandfather was living with us, had been teaching me to drive, and was an active part of my life. One really cold winter night, my grandfather wasn't feeling well. He was rushed to the hospital where days later he passed away. I was 17 years old when my grandfather transitioned, and it was at that moment that

I told my grandmother I had to make it to heaven. The only solace I had after all these blows to my heart was the scripture in 1 Thessalonians 4:13-14: "...you will not grieve like people who have no hope. For since we believe that Jesus died and was raised to life again, we also believe that when Jesus returns, God will bring back with him the believers who have died." This was the determination that hit me on that day, that no matter what happens, there is nothing worse than losing the people you love dearly. I had made up my mind that I was going to follow Jesus so I could see my loved ones in heaven one day.

This initial conviction jumpstarted my Yes journey with the Lord. I wanted to say Yes to Him, even if I didn't really understand what that meant. I knew at my core I wanted God. If you can't recount the moment when you came into agreement with the crossroad God took you on to follow Him, you might not have had that experience yet. You might have an experience like Paul who was going in a totally different direction when Jesus encountered him on the road to Damascus. He was blinded, then God opened his eyes to his new life. It was that encounter that persuaded Paul to follow Christ. Pain is often the birthing place for purpose, and that area of purpose is the well of prosperity. Your wealth is tied to your purpose, but you will never experience the fullness of your purpose if you run from the pain. The pain is needed to push you from the attachment to this earthly world to the realization that we are just passing by here, and this is not our home.

The real Yes that God wants from us is a Yes for eternity. The type of Yes that says, "For the rest of my

The Imprint of a Yes

days I will serve the Lord. Regardless of what life sends my way, I will never stop following him. No matter if I experience heartache or heartbreak, disappointment, or shame, I will not stop choosing God. I am in His hands and He has the authority to do whatever He wishes to do with this life, and I offer Him no resistance. I actively submit to the way and the will God has for me." But this decidedness is birthed through experiences of pain. But the pain isn't meant to kill you but transcend you to another level in God. The pain takes you from your idea to God's idea. It derails you from your way to God's way. The pain we go through is not designed to take us away from the Father but draw us closer to Him. The enemy would try to convince you that these platforms of pain are meant to destroy you. But you won't experience your platform increase if you have a low tolerance for pain. It's the pain that stretches your platform. The greater the pain capacity you have, the more God can trust you with an increased influence. Jesus had to endure the ultimate pain to receive the ultimate reward.

What you have gone through, and the healing God is taking you through, is for a reach far greater than your friends list on Facebook and your followers on Instagram. There are people all over in places you have never been that need your story and history with God. They need to know that God can deliver you from an abusive relationship and that you can recover it all by starting afresh because He did it for you. You must allow the determination in your Yes to be so real that you won't allow shame to keep you muzzled from sharing the facts of your story. The facts might be that you had to file for bankruptcy after experiencing a bad divorce, but the truth is that God makes all things new, and can breathe on something that was once dead and give it new life because He did it in you.

There have been too many G-rated stories out here because people are ashamed of the R-rating their story really is. But there is no shame in the redemption of God. If God has forgiven you and given you a new start, there is no one on earth or in hell who can condemn you for a past that Jesus has covered under the blood. Your story needs to be shared. The scripture tells us that we overcome by the blood of the lamb and the word of our testimony. The testimony is essential in the power of the blood being displayed. The testimony says, "I was guilty of the sin I was committing, but His blood took the curse away from me, and I can now live in Him freely." You don't have to live in shame because of poor decisions of your past when you were struggling with receiving the love of God. We sin when we are trying to fill the voids, we experience with anything that isn't the love of God. When you have received the love of God, you won't run to substances to numb the pain, but running into Jesus gives you the peace you are looking for.

When you stop wrestling with the love of God, your soul will yield a determined Yes to the Lord. When you wrestle with His love, you are fighting against the truth that the thoughts God thinks towards you are good and not evil, to give you an expected end. God is not trying to figure out what He will do with your life if you say yes. He has already mapped it out. He is just waiting on you to be determined to stay on the path and

The Imprint of a Yes

follow through on the course of the Yes being embedded into you. This process takes time and it will require you to take ownership of your part in the journey. You may not be the one who leads the venture, but there are responsibilities you have to steward well. God won't make you process through healing. He won't force you to forgive and He won't force you to find accountability. If you truly desire to take the forever journey with God, you will need to yield to Him so He can staff your life with accountability. This could be a person, group, or community that has the same mind you have, which is to stay in the process with the Lord.

You need to be surrounded by like-minded people. They say you are the five closest people to you. If you look at your circle right now, what type of people would you see around you? Are the people in your inner circle people who do just enough to say they did it? Are they lazy and unreliable? Are the people around you in cycles of sin and complacent with poverty? You, my friend, might be in agreement with the type of people you have around you. The type of people you need in your circle as you are being processed and refined are people who have unwavering faith in God. These are the people who radically believe that God will do exactly what He says. You also need the type of individual who has business acumen. God created us to be self-governed; this is the will of God for us, to live our lives in a way we govern ourselves, according to the Kingdom in which we have citizenship.

You need to know how to run a business, no matter if you feel called to entrepreneurship or not. God has called you to have dominion, and you need to know how to manage that dominion. You also need someone who is good with money management. This is important because you need to learn how to steward the finances God gives you, so you can multiply what He places in your hands. God gives seed to the sower. If we follow the principles God gave us, we should be able to receive anything from the Lord and multiply that using the treasure He has placed inside our earthen vessel. The soul is where your wealth is locked up. When you have the right community around you, there is support to help you stay in the process. Yet there is a level of inward decision we all must have to become all that God has called us to be. A community is not to be used as a crutch, or for trauma bonding, but to keep the standard before your eyes.

It takes a level of vulnerability to share with someone the vision you believe God has given you. This is why you must choose your community intentionally. We are not perfect, but we should all yield to the perfecting process of God. As your life is staffed for the various seasons God will lead you into, it is your responsibility to steward them well and not commonly. These people have been hand-chosen by God to assist you in your season. If you have been betrayed by people in your past, you must allow the Holy Spirit to heal those parts of your soul that would speak inner vows like "I will never trust again" or "I will never let anyone in close." These words will be like barricades from the people destined to come into your life. Allow the Holy Spirit to heal you, so you can see the help and not hurt the help. God will assign people to your life who have the capacity to hear your vulnerability and store it like a vault, like God-ordained safe spaces. These people remind you of your Yes and encourage you to keep going when you feel like giving up.

Godly accountability can be a lifeline in the midst of giving up. Accountability, if used properly, will keep you from stumbling. But you have to reach out to accountability before you fall into the different temptations, not after. Accountability isn't a confessional. It is to help keep you on track. Accountability is for a season like training wheels is for a bicycle. When a child is learning to ride a bike for the first time, they get training wheels on the back to help keep them balanced while they learn the motion the bike rides in. But after a while, the child no longer needs training wheels but is ready to take them off and ride without additional assistance. This doesn't mean they won't fall off the bike from time to time. But it won't keep them from riding the bike in the future. They learn from the fall, they adjust, and they move forward.

Your decision to begin the process is the start. Then you have to be disciplined in the decision of the process. Then find the accountability you need to keep you truthful to the process, to end up fortifying your decision with your time in devotion to God. Your devotion time with God strengthens what He said to you. It's the time in devotion when God will tell you about yourself and what He has planned for you. It's in devotion that God builds up your spirit man to make spiritual decisions. Don't despise the time of devotion; I believe it's the most important portion of your decided Yes. When I am unsure of the future, God reveals to me His plans in devotion. But you will miss out on insight and secrets if you don't take the time to be in His presence.

When you have life-changing encounters, it births a determination inside you to choose what you want your life to look like. You can determine to follow the way of the Spirit and receive the reward of walking in the Spirit. Or you can make choices that will lead you to live a life under the privilege of being a son or daughter of God. What would that be like, to live a life for however long the good Lord gives you, just to end it and never accomplish or experience the purpose of why God sent you here? Could you imagine after 75 or 90 years that you close your eyes on time and wake up in eternity, and God tells you that there was so much more that He had in store for you, but you wouldn't tell Him Yes? That after all the time you could have agreed with the plans of God for your life, you chose to take the safe route in life and experience 80 years of a basic life?

We must value the sacrifice of Jesus so much until we partner with Him for the abundant life that comes from a decided life of partnership with the Holy Spirit. We have one life on this side of eternity, and what you do today will determine what type of floor the generations after you will have. What are you doing today that will make your children's and grandchildren's life better? What yes have you come into agreement with that will yield a harvest for generations after you to eat from? If you seize these moments and follow the direction of the Holy Spirit, your ceiling will be your children's floor, and they will be able to experience the benefits of your labor and take the legacy even further for the generations to come.

The Imprint of a Yes

Your Yes has the power to change your bloodline for generations to come. Your agreement in the earth is that serious to heaven. Decide in your mind today that you will have a determined Yes and that no matter what will happen in your lifetime, your answer to the Lord will be an emphatic Yes.

Chapter 4

Hold On Tight

There's a story shared in 2 Samuel 23:9-10 about one of David's mighty men of valor named Eleazar. He was a skillful elite warrior. The scripture tells us about a time when Eleazar was in battle against the Philistines. Because Israel retreated, he remained there and singlehandedly killed those Philistines. He fought until his hand was too tired to hold up, but he never stopped fighting. The story is told that the Lord gave him a great victory that day, and Israel came back only to collect the spoils.

The Imprint of a Yes

At that time the handle of a sword was usually wrapped in a leather-type material or rope-like covering. Eleazar had his hand on the handle of his weapon for so long, as you could imagine, when the sword was ripped from his hand the imprint of the handle was pressed in.

As you partner with the Holy Spirit in the actions of your faith which say Yes to God, you must be like this skilled warrior. He was so determined not to lose the fight that he continued to do so even when his body was trying to fail him. Something supernatural took over him for him to have gone to his last swing to being victorious in battle. What if God sent an angel to help fight with him? The tightness of the grasp from the supernatural into the natural would leave a dent that was undeniable. Giving God a Yes will cause you to fight in a time when there may not be anyone around you to help. Yet if you have a mindset that says, "It doesn't matter how long it takes, I won't stop fighting," the power of the Holy Ghost can begin to work on our behalf. The scripture tells us that "it's in our weakness that His strength is made perfect" (2 Corinthians 12). We have to work and do all we can, with all the strength we have, until there is nothing left but for God to step in.

Keep holding on! The fight may seem like it's never-ending, but don't stop fighting. On the other side is a story that can be shared about the partnering power of God. He will allow you to do the supernatural even when you have no natural energy or strength left. Hold on tight to what God said. Believe His word for your life so much that it imprints in your ear and unto your heart. You might not have a physical imprint on your hand, but let your agreement to His plan be something you hold on to.

Have you ever experienced a time when God spoke to you prophetically about your future? Or have you had a person be used prophetically by God to speak His plan to your heart? When these words from the Lord come, they are meant to be taken seriously and to heart. This is why you hold on to the word and watch God perform it. However, if we don't hold on to the word, we can miss out on an opportunity to see God manifest Himself in the earth.

Holding on can hurt. It can cause fluids to be rushed to the place of discomfort in an attempt to alleviate the pressure. The water of

The Imprint of a Yes

God is meant to do the same. It's there to send a cushion to be around your heart, so when an adversary comes it won't be able to cause a direct blow to the heart, because it has fluid around it as protection. The fluid may cause an imprint to be shown when it's under pressure, but that's an indication that what was being held had been transferred to the one holding it. It's not good enough just to have the promise of God in your head, but it needs to be engrafted in your heart. The Holy Spirit is like the water in your body. It can go wherever the healing is needed. The Holy Spirit can go into battle, and it can go to the places that need comfort. Build a relationship with the Holy Spirit because, without Him, you won't have the power to endure or last. But He is the keeper. The Holy Spirit is the portion of God's spirit that helps us while on earth to accomplish the greater things Jesus spoke about. Make Him real to you as you are reading this book. The Holy Spirit wants to be your sustainer and your strength.

The process of living out the Yes you gave to God comes with a permanent price. It's like getting a tattoo. The tattoo artist has the image which is being transferred from paper to the body. Once the image is adhered to the desired place, the ink-filled needle starts the process of engraving. It can be uncomfortable to sit there with the humming of the needle gun and the repetition of the needle going back and forth, digging into the skin to ensure the ink is going in deep enough to penetrate through. After the work is complete, the area around the new tattoo is red, irritated, and often inflamed. This doesn't mean the engraving wasn't administered correctly; it just means it needs time to heal. Then once healed, the redness disappears and the swelling goes down. It doesn't become permanent after the healing takes place, but rather from the moment the tattoo artist places the needle on the skin. If God has called you to do anything for the advancement of His Kingdom, no matter if that's starting a business, opening a school, feeding the homeless, or preaching the gospel, you must be certain and decide that you will do it. If you come into agreement that you will accomplish the task, God will give you all the supernatural energy and strength you need to conquer it. He will send resources and connections, partnerships, and referrals. But you have to keep holding on until what is in your hand transfers to being imprinted in your heart.

Chapter 5

A Generational Yes

My great-great-grandmother was Vassie Lean Cunningham. She married Jeff Robinson and had nine children: two boys and seven girls. Vassie Lean was a sharecropper who traveled with the season. She was known to be a praying woman who loved her family. She raised her children to pray and to live a life that was reflected in being set aside. I was told stories as a child about how she would pray for her children and her children's children. She had a heart that led her to pray into a future that was yet unborn. She would often pray for their salvation, and for them to know the Lord. As she got older, she passed the baton over to her daughters. The Robinson girls were the seven prophetesses of their time. Six of the sisters were church helpers and built up their local assemblies.

However, there was one sister who was led to a higher calling. Matthew 22:14 says, "For many are called, but few are chosen." This sister's name was Ethel Lee Robinson, affectionately called "Teeny." God had called her to do something that had not been done before in my family's history: move from Delaware to California. She would be the first member of the Robinson clan to live that far away. But Ethel Lee was on an assignment by God. She was called to the nations. She lived the life she was taught by her mother. To pray without ceasing, to be a help to the needy, and to be obedient to what God tells her to do. Ethel Lee was my great-grandmother, and I can recall her praying for her children and their children's children. I saw her give God a Yes with her life. There were times that she would get phone calls all throughout the night from people asking for prayer requests from all around the world.

When God called my great-grandmother to nations, it didn't look how it may look today. She did not have any internet access; they didn't have Zoom or WhatsApp. She would work as a prayer partner for Trinity Broadcasting Network (TBN), one of the largest

Christian networks at that time. She would pray for people all over the world who would call in. Ethel Lee was dedicated to her prayer assignment. She instilled in her family the importance of having a relationship with God, even when it takes you to uncharted territory. Ethel Lee had two children: Vassie Anne and James Henry Mills. She taught my Grandmother Vassie Anne that the journey of a prophet is a lonely journey and that there are times when you will be misunderstood, disliked, criticized, betrayed, mishandled, and overlooked. But no matter what people may try to do to you, pray for them and forgive them swiftly. My grandmother instilled this in me as well.

When you are living a life that says Yes to God, it has the reach of at least a hundred years. The Yes that my great-great-grandmother made to God set up a path for the generations to come. Her Yes doesn't mean that I did not have to say Yes; however, it showed me that if I gave God a Yes, my great-great-grandchildren would be able to reap the benefit of saying Yes to God. It is an honor to be chosen by God. To be able to hear His voice and respond. It is not something that should be taken lightly. The God who created the universe, the God who has always been and will always be, called your name from eternity into time. I appreciate my ancestors, but I don't pray to them. God will not allow any other gods to be placed before Him, because all other gods are made by humans, and He created the human. When you are living out your Yes, you can't afford to have a spiritual mixture in your heart.

For your Yes to be generational, we must put everything into perspective. God is meant to be in a space all by Himself as the Creator of all. Then our ancestors are in the place of appreciation for the sacrifices they made. Because if they did not contend for their life, they would not have a future, which are the descendants who came after them. We don't worship the ancestors; we worship the God of our ancestors. I knew exactly what God my family believed in. I have had to learn Him in my own personal way, but I can see that He is trustworthy because my bloodline has a track record with Him. The power that's behind the generational mantles passed down isn't in the mantle alone, but the fact that God has been there from the very beginning and has not failed them. So, if He didn't fail them, He won't start with me. It is important that you impart this to your children and the ones you oversee your history with God.

I can have confidence that my future is secure in Him, because the scripture says in Jeremiah 29:11, "For I know the plans I have for you says the Lord. They are plans for good and not disaster, to give you a future and a hope." This scripture is then confirmed by the history and testimony my great-grandmother and grandmother had. Therefore, as I look out on life, and it seems like the days are getting darker, I can have confidence that the God of Vassie Lean, Ethel Lee, and Vassie Anne is with me and that the thoughts He thinks towards me are good. I know they are good because down through the years, I have eyewitness accounts from my ancestors of the faithfulness of God. Even if you don't know if you had any grandparents who said Yes to God, or maybe you did not grow up in church at all, that is okay. You have the opportunity to change the history with your bloodline for the next hundred years if you simply give God a lifelong Yes. The Yes, my predecessors gave wasn't just a one-time Yes, but a Yes that lasts into eternity.

The Imprint of a Yes

Now that the benefits of their Yes have been passed down to me and for generations to come, my bloodline will have an example of what it looks like to live a life that says Yes to God.

What you choose to do today will determine what your future holds for tomorrow. You get to make a choice to partner with eternity for a life that will be a benefit for the time to come. When you come into agreement with the God of your predecessors, you come into agreement with the plans and purpose He has for you, and the ones to come after you. This doesn't mean that every day will be easy or perfect. But this does mean that you will be able to labor and reap a benefit from it. If you submit to the will and way of God and allow it to play out in your life, you will be able to experience heaven on earth. But you have to choose to take God's way. He will not allow you to only drink from a bitter cup, and you not experience the taste of the sweetness of being obedient. I am reminded of Psalm 34:8 (Passion Translation): "Drink deeply of the pleasures of this God. Experience for yourself the joyous mercies he gives to all who turn to hide themselves in him." Hiding yourself in God is a conscious decision to live in Him. This cannot be done if you don't give God a Yes. This means when someone mistreats you, you chose to let God vindicate you. When others don't choose you to lead a task, you choose to let God give you an assignment. Hiding in Him isn't for you but for the ones after you. It shows them what it looks like to be submitted to God. Will you be the example of a life that says Yes to God? Will you be the plot twist in your bloodline that becomes the reason your family experiences generational blessings? We all must make the decision to say Yes to God. But when someone else has said it, it helps others have a light to see the direction to go in.

I was taught that the way is lonely because it is narrow, it's not the most glamorous way, and it's not a way that is self-pleasing and self-exalting, so not many go that way. However, God can send you a community of people on the narrow path. This doesn't mean it will be a multitude of people; it might be just one family, group, or ministry. It won't be perfect, but all you need is a Yes to the perfecting. When our time expires here on earth, we will be transitioned into eternity. On the other side of our earthly Yes is a heavenly

Yes. The only way for you to experience the Yes of God after we take our last breath is if we give Jesus a heartfelt Yes. He's not looking for you to have it all together. He's not looking for you to know all the answers. All He is looking for is for you to come into agreement with His good and perfect plan for your life. You might not see it revealed in the first portion of your life, but if you continue to journey with Him, you will eventually see the goodness of the Lord in the land of the living. The goodness will be so good that you will see it with your natural eye, and your descendants will witness it with theirs and hear it with their ears. The Holy One doesn't just want to be your God, but the God of your children's children. Stay on the path with Him, no matter what comes your way, and let God imprint the Yes.

Made in the USA
Middletown, DE
09 March 2024